Love

REIKI

vibration

Love REIKI vibration

guidance for the modern-day wellness warrior

CORTNEY MARTINELLI

Book design by Cortney Martinelli.
Editing by Heather Ninni.
Printed in the United States of America.
First printing, 2018.

SHINE Akron LLC
5190 Cline Rd
Kent, Oh 44240
www.shineakron.com

I dedicate this book to my Reiki students.
Also, Nicole Woodford-Shell, who renewed my passion for teaching, community and life.
Lastly, my son, Zach, who saved my soul.

Three things
can not be long hidden;
the sun,
the moon,
and the truth.

Buddha

Contents

Part 3 - Rapid-Fire Practical Advice on Hot Topics

Graphics

Introduction

Are you a modern-day wellness warrior? I'd say you most certainly are, especially if you have been attracted to this book. You are holding it in your hands right now for a reason. I've seen a trend lately towards people taking charge of their own wellbeing. As seen with the big boom of essential oils and yoga studios popping up on every corner, the increased awareness and consumption of organic and non-processed foods, and the growing number of Reiki practitioners. This makes me giddy. I'm willing to indulge the idea that maybe this is only in my corner of the world, but you are reading this, so that means you are part of that world too.

Sometimes, this need to take charge of our health comes from a last-resort-mentality. Maybe you or someone you know has landed at a crossroads, one where you no longer have the luxury of leading the same old, unhealthy life. The stress and anxiety have finally manifested into something physical and the point has been reached where you must find an alternative to the life you have been living. This is what happened to me. As I type this, I am grateful to realize that it feels like a lifetime ago. In fact, it's almost impossible for me to reach for those desperate feelings that once seemed so normal. What I'm saying is...there's hope!! Regardless of whether you are a new wellness warrior, or have been on this path for years, this book will offer the guidance you seek. I promise.

Why this book, why now

In 2010, I had my first Reiki session and, shortly after, I became a Reiki practitioner as a way to begin my own healing process. At the time, I couldn't know the full implications of taking that first step. Almost ten years later, leading up to my 42nd birthday, I decided that I would finally put down on paper the knowledge and experiences I have collected since that fateful day in March of 2010.

This book contains:

The things that I have learned over the last decade.

Those things I have learned from personal experiences; not from books or manuals.

The things that resonate most with my students.

The ahas that have risen out of conversations with others.

The things that I say out loud and then think to myself, "Where did that come from?"...especially those things.

The things that have changed my practice, my spiritual journey, my students' journeys, my life, and the lives of those I co-create with.

Some might think Reiki is magical.

Some might think it saved their life.

Some might think it is weird.

Some might think it is bologna.

Some might have experienced it, yet, still are at a loss for what it is.

And some - like me - have seen it, experienced it, given it, taught it, lived it, and with heart-wide-open – fell in love with it.

I honor all these perspectives.

But for me, it was love at first sight.

I've said for years that I am not in the business of convincing anyone of anything – and that still holds true. This book is for those who already hold the truth deep down inside of them and are looking for a catalyst to bring it out. You (yes, I actually mean YOU, the person holding this book) are the co-creator of this book; you are the one that has called these words onto paper. As we will soon explore, we are all connected. And this book has been written through me and for you. Yes, the main topic is Reiki, but anyone who is interested in finding deeper meaning about their health and wellbeing can glean value.

Let me explain

I set out to write a book about Reiki. As the book unfolded, two other themes emerged: love and vibration. On the surface, this book is a guide to Reiki, but the deeper truths are universal. To give you an idea, this book – *Love, Reiki, Vibration* - contains the word **Reiki** 286 times, the word **love** 62 times, and the word **vibration** 61 times.

I invite you to consider the following before jumping in...

Stay in your head and you're dead. Some of what is written here isn't for the analytical mind. Let me assure you, I know what it's like to be stuck in my head. I am an analytical person. My bachelor's degree is in accounting and I get excited when people start talking about spreadsheets (ha!). I am the definition of type A. I lived the first 30 years of my life leading with my left brain. So, trust me when I say that sometimes you have to listen with your heart. If you don't have a single aha or don't feel some sort of shift after reading this book, it's possible you've remained in your head the entire time.

Keep an open mind and an open heart. One of my friends would always say to me, a book is like a buffet; there's lots to choose from, some dishes you might not like (maybe too spicy, too salty, or too bland) and others you might go back for seconds or thirds. By all means, fill-up on what you're hungry for! However, I hope, regardless of your current beliefs, that you can keep an open mind and an open heart when exploring the pages of this book. You were drawn to this book for a reason. You need to find out why. And that reason might surprise you. If you are reading a page, a chapter, or even the entire book and it starts to resemble the sound of Charlie Brown's teacher, then you might not be ready to hear what it has to say. Tuck it away and bring it out later. My favorite book is the Tao and each time I read it, I hear something different. The book *hasn't* changed. I have.

The first two chapters are foundational for understanding the rest of the book, so skipping past them is not recommended. In fact, each word, each sentence, each chapter has been deliberately designed. Each is a piece of the puzzle, and at the end, you will arrive at your own truth. It will unfold perfectly and uniquely for you.

Keep an eye out for italicized words or phrases; there is an intended emphasis where they appear.

In this book, I use the words Source or Divine in place of the word God. Feel free to use whichever word feels right to you. This book is for you, and I would hate for semantics to be a sticking point.

Lastly, I've bared my soul within this book. It's about what I've learned from my experiences over the last decade. If I've said anything in this book that offends you, please know that was never my intention. If I've said something that is different from what you believe or what you have experienced, I find solace in knowing there is room in this world for both points-of-view, and I honor and celebrate our differences as much as our likeness.

Now we're ready. Let's start from the beginning.

PART 1

Love, Reiki, Vibration

Enter at your own risk,
this book was written for the warrior

CHAPTER 1

One connected to the Source is more powerful than a million who are not.

What is Reiki

Reiki (ray-key) can be a little tricky to explain. After all, you can't see it. It's not tangible. I've had people approach me at events and tell me that although they have taken Reiki training, received the attunement, and maybe even practiced on clients – they still aren't sure *what* it is. I've spent the last few years of my Reiki career trying to take this esoteric concept and make it more accessible to others. It might be easiest to start with the *word* itself; what is the meaning of the word Reiki?

The word Reiki comes from two Japanese words and is loosely translated to mean, life-force energy guided by Source. *Rei* meaning Source, a higher consciousness, God, the Divine – call it what you will, it all means the same. Ki meaning energy. In the Chinese culture we call this energy Chi. In yoga, we call it Prana. In church we call it Spirit...it all means the same thing. It is the energy that animates us all. That which gives us life on this *physical* plain. That which breathes us.

So, there we are. When we talk about Reiki, we are talking about life-force energy guided by a higher power. This is the same energy that creates worlds. As you can imagine, it *is* quite

TWO JAPANESE WORDS

REI + KI

higher consciousness   *life force energy*

magical. Magical, yet, ordinary at the same time. Einstein said, "There are only two ways to live your life: as though nothing is a miracle, or as though everything is a miracle." The same goes for Reiki, you get to decide. But still, after hearing this explanation, you are probably no closer to the truth. You may be shaking your head and looking to me for more explanation.

We are energy

It might humble you to know that everything in this universe is 99.999 percent empty space. This is, scientifically speaking, because we are made up of atoms and atoms are 99.999 percent empty space. It's hard to fathom this in our minds. I like to use the image of a football stadium to help fully grasp the magnitude of this concept. Imagine an atom magnified to the size of a football stadium. The nucleus of the atom would be the size of a pea in the center of the stadium, and the electrons would be whizzing around the outer stands. Everything in between is *empty space.*

That's a lot of empty space. It's been said that if a human were to lose the empty space between her atoms, she could fit into a spec of dust and the entire human race could fit into a teaspoon. A freakin' teaspoon, people!

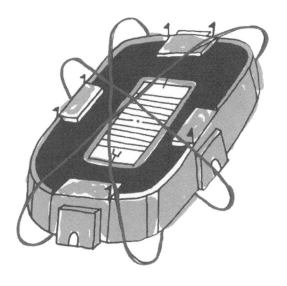

Ah, but this empty space isn't really 'empty.'
This empty space is energy.
This energy is spiritual.
This spiritual energy animates all things.
And Reiki can and does affect it.

Reiki raises your vibration

Energy = vibration. Einstein said, "Everything in life is vibration." What he meant is that every atom in every molecule oscillates and is in motion. Our physical bodies are made of energy and are vibrating at *different* frequencies. My frequency is different than yours. Your frequency is different than your parents. Your parents' frequencies are different than their neighbors...so on and so forth.

Hang in there with me. This is where it starts getting good.

Scientists can measure this vibration.

What we know from scientific studies is that the frequency of a healthy human body lies within 62 to 72 MHz. When a human body's frequency begins to drop to somewhere in the range of 57 to 60 MHz, the body becomes receptive to colds and flus. A frequency below 58 MHz makes the body receptive to disease; specifically cancer at 42 MHz and below. They say that death begins occurring at 25 MHz. The chart to follow will help you visualize this.

Here's the golden nugget, get your highlighter ready...

In theory, if we keep the frequency of our body above 62 MHz, diseases and harmful bacteria would have a very hard time surviving in our body.

You might be thinking, where does Reiki come into play with all this *sciency* talk? Reiki *raises* the vibration of the human body. (Mic drop.) That's a holy crap moment! Imagine the implications. If *your* body is vibrating below 62 MHz due to stress, anxiety, poor quality fuel, negative thinking – whatever the reason – performing Reiki on yourself can counteract this and raise your personal frequency (vibration). It can restore balance back to your body. I can't imagine one single person on Earth that couldn't benefit from this.

Likely, you have manifested and/or are now experiencing physical ailments based on your current vibration – some manifestations may be more serious than others – however,

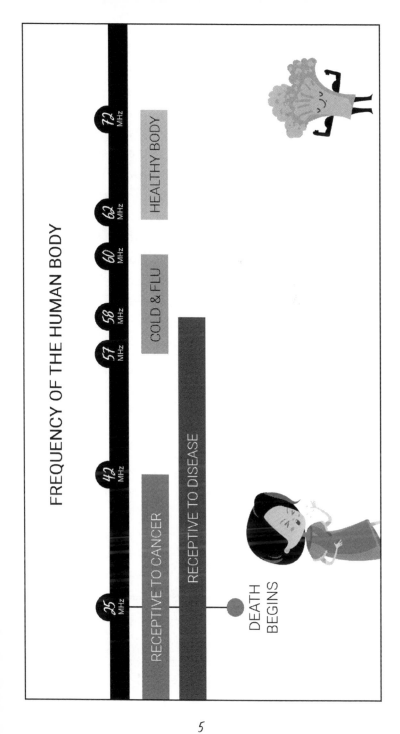

know that by increasing your vibration through Reiki (and other high-flying lifestyle choices talked about in Chapter 4 and as shown on page 87), you can begin vibrating at the level of a healthy body.

Now, this of course doesn't mean that you should stop any treatment you are currently doing. It's to emphasis the fact that once the human body vibrates *consistently* at a certain level, the body takes care of itself without outside assistance.

And this, my friends, is why Reiki is indeed magical. It is one of the best ways to kick-start someone's wellbeing. This is the reason why when I test the chakras - after a Reiki session - they are all open (more in Chapter 8) because I have just spent the last 60 minutes raising the vibration of my client. It never ceases to amaze me. Each time I am in awe. If you've experienced it, I am sure you are in awe too.

Reiki, how is it different from other healing

The answer is: it's not. It's not different from any other healing. To heal is to raise your vibration. You can do this in hundreds, if not thousands of ways. (PS – you can also lower your vibration in hundreds, if not thousands of ways.) But I can sum up the ways we raise and lower our vibration in two simple words.

Love. Fear.

Love raises our vibration.

Fear lowers our vibration.

As the *Course in Miracles* beautifully states, "Every choice you make is either an expression of love or an expression of fear. There is no other choice."

Reiki is love. Love is Reiki.

What's up with the attunements

An attunement is how one receives and accesses (for a lack of a better word) the Reiki energy.

Reiki is transferred during an attunement process from an experienced Reiki Master to a student. During the attunement process, a couple of things are occurring within the student. First and foremost, the student is being connected to the Reiki source. Also, alterations are being made in the student's energy pathways to accommodate the changes needed for Reiki. After having an attunement (there is more than one, and we talk about this in detail in Chapter 3), you are considered a Reiki practitioner.

Attunements are beautiful and magical; I equate it to being wrapped in a blanket of unconditional love and feeling completely supported and safe. It's what I imagine the gaze of the Divine feels like, in all of its glory.

I once had a beautiful soul ask me, "If we are all from and part of the Source, aren't we already connected to the Reiki source? Why is there even a need for an attunement?" I share this question with you here, because some of you might be thinking the very same thing.

Here's what I believe...

I believe, as stated above, that there are many ways to heal. It comes down to four letters: l-o-v-e. I believe that we can heal with love, the power of prayer, our words, our thoughts, our touch, our intentions. We are all connected and therefore can affect the personal frequency (vibration) of one another. Reiki is simply one of the hundreds of ways to heal (i.e. raise vibration). This particular way, brought into life by Dr. Usui in 1914, uses an attunement process to connect you to the source of Reiki. It doesn't mean without it you aren't connected to *the* Source or that you can't already heal yourself or others. Reiki is just another avenue to access our true nature. The true nature that is within every being. Reiki supports the realization of this true nature.

To sum it up, Reiki is just *another* tool that one can use to raise the vibration of oneself or another to bring about healing.

Or...

is it more?

Reiki is a lifestyle

Let's take it one step further, Reiki is a lifestyle.

Sure, Reiki is often packaged as a one-hour session where a person lays on a massage table and a Reiki practitioner gently 'lays hands on' usually using a standard set of hand positions. It's true – this is Reiki. I have had hundreds, if not thousands of these one-on-one sessions with clients. However, it is only a small part of Reiki. Just like a yoga class is only a small part of yoga. (Where are my yogis at?) A true Reiki practitioner is one who allows the 'life-force energy, guided by Source' to fill every nook and cranny of her life.

There isn't an aspect of my life that isn't touched by Reiki (no pun intended). If you are a Reiki practitioner and you haven't yet considered this, please keep an open mind as we explore this topic in more detail throughout the rest of the book.

As we close out this chapter about *What is Reiki*, this is the perfect time to say...Reiki is available to all. Both the giving and receiving of Reiki is obtainable without discrimination. Regardless of your age, gender, race, religious background, status, intellectual capacity, lifestyle choices, preferences, and spiritual development – Reiki flows freely.

CHAPTER 2

*At the core, a healer is someone who has the
ability to raise vibration. It's that simple.*

What is a healer

It's not possible to talk about Reiki without defining what it means to be a healer.

Every Reiki Master has a unique approach and style to teaching Reiki; it is the sum of their beliefs and life experiences. Since we all have different beliefs and life experiences, it makes each Reiki Master unique; it makes each Reiki class unique. I believe we are drawn to the people that teach what resonates with us. We are literally attracted to them, like a magnet. I humbly share with you now the root of my teachings, and it has everything to do with my definition of a healer.

At the core, *a healer is someone who has the ability to raise vibration.* It's that simple.

Sometimes this is done intentionally and sometimes we do it without realizing it. There are people in every profession that I would consider healers.

There are school teachers speaking faith into their students – they are healers.

There are CEOs and business leaders empowering employees to add meaning to the world's economy – they are healers.

There are yoga teachers holding space for students to dive deep into their inner world – they are healers.

There are poets, song writers, authors, painters, and dancers creating beautiful works of art and sharing their soul with the world – they are healers.

I am certain that if you closed your eyes and thought about it for a second, you could think of one, two, even several people that you interact with throughout your week that raise your vibration. You may not have thought of it in this way before, but you certainly have experienced interacting with someone who made you feel better, lighter, and happier. *They raised your vibration*; they contributed to your wellbeing; they are a healer. And of course, you have probably experienced the opposite; people who have lowered your vibration. Sometimes we call these people energy-vampires, buzz-killers, and devil's advocates (I'm keeping it clean here). This person is the opposite of a healer. But, just like in my life, I will not concern myself with them here; instead we will dive deeper into the traits of a healer.

Traits of a true healer

I believe there are two distinct traits that enable someone to heal. I will explain each trait in detail.

A healer inspires a reduction of resistance in others. Usually a healer does this while loving the person where he is, exactly how he is, seeing the person through the eyes of Source and knowing that she is perfect and whole just as she is in this very moment. I tell my Reiki students, that one of the most important things they can do when working with others is to create an environment that is conducive to *releasing resistance.* You can do this by making your clients as comfortable as possible. Whether that is through preparing them before-hand for what to expect; easing their mind about how the session will unfold; offering a suitable mantra for them to focus on during your time together; providing a comfortable room and place for them to lay where the temperature is just-right; diffusing essential oils that they find to be relaxing and pleasant; or playing music that they enjoy and that is not distracting. These outer elements contribute to creating an environment where they can easily release internal resistance. Each one of the elements I mention above can raise the vibration of a human body all on its own.

More importantly, however, is the preparation of your internal state before working with a client. A healer must tend to their own personal frequency regularly. After all, your client can pick up on your energy subconsciously. Your energy can set the tone for a calm and relaxing interaction. The goal here is to soothe them – to be a catalyst and assist them as they open to the receiving of what they desire.

A healer holds the space of wellbeing for another. I never, ever, never, ever want to focus on my client's 'illness' or 'problem', never! So regardless of what a client shares with me regarding their health before a session, I focus on their wellbeing. This is one of the most important concepts in this entire book.

Understand what is going on here. Let's assume that *most* of the time, your clients are coming to you because they have something 'wrong' with them. I can guarantee that this problem consumes most of their thoughts. In fact, universal law ensures this. Someone must hold the space of wellbeing for them. Someone *must* focus on their true nature, their perfection, their wholeness, their wellbeing, the idea that their cells are regenerating constantly. AND I assure you, it's not going to be them – so it *must* be you.

If you get really good at this, you will have people lining up to be in your presence. In fact, this is ultimately what Jesus did. People would stand in front of Jesus, dripping in their illness, and he would look at them through the eyes of the Father and know their wholeness, know their perfection, know their divinity, know their birth-right. This is the space where miracles happen. This is how you raise vibration. This is how you heal.

Of course, there are implications of focusing on your *own* illness and your *own* problems too. I save this discussion for Chapter 12. It's a good one.

In truth, you can't heal anyone but yourself. You can only support the healing of others. The work is always to close the gap. The gap is always internal; never external. The external is only a reflection. Start supporting others by first taking care of your internal gap.

Taking care of yourself first

It is said that Mrs. Takata, the person responsible for bringing Reiki from Japan to the West, would tell her students, "Reiki you first." She understood the importance of being aligned and balanced before offering the gift of Reiki to another. We've all heard the sayings; place the oxygen mask on yourself first before helping others; you can't pour from an empty cup; always wear clean underwear, you never know when you'll end up in the ER. Ok, that last one doesn't really fit here, just making sure you are paying attention. I digressed. As a Reiki practitioner who is caring for others, I can tell you that this practice of taking care of yourself is so important. If you don't have a high vibration, by universal law, you cannot contribute to the high vibration of another. It is simply impossible. Consider taking a moment, right now, by putting the book down and reflecting on whether you are taking care of yourself or not. Do you have a high vibration? A vibration high enough that will allow you the liberty of offering it to another. I'll stop talking for a sec while you think about that for a moment. (pause for reflection ♡)

In recent years, studies have confirmed the ripple effect of happiness. Taking care of one's self and investing in your wellbeing can be contagious and spread beyond your immediate circles. It can spread through clusters of people who may not even know each other. Not to mention, the effect it can have on your significant other, your children, your co-workers, your friends, and all of those you interact with on a daily basis. Alignment is what we are all reaching for. When we see someone who is aligned with their true power (which is ultimately how I define happiness), it inspires us to be aligned too. Check out the graphic on the following page that illustrates this ripple effect.

Dr Usui, the founder of Reiki, offers a suggestion for alignment through a meditation he refers to as Gassho. Usui called this technique the first pillar of Reiki (first pillar – it's that important my friend) and he practiced it twice a day. Gassho means 'two-hands coming together' and it can be used to clear the mind, open the heart, and strengthen one's Reiki energy.

At a minimum, I recommend to my students that they use the technique right before laying hands on a client for a session.

Gassho is simple...let's practice it now.

Fold your hands in prayer position with your fingers pointing up and your thumbs touching your heart.

Focus your attention on the point where your middle fingers meet.

Put slightly more pressure on the middle fingers as you press them together with ease.

With any form of meditation, your mind will beg for attention, but continue to bring your attention back to the middle fingers.

Now, close your eyes while practicing for a few moments.

It's that simple.

The benefits, of course, show up after it becomes a habit. In fact, after using this technique while preparing for clients over the last decade, it now triggers a deep state of consciousness within me almost instantly.

Of course, there are many ways to take care of yourself and meditation is just one. It's all about choosing consistent lifestyle choices that will raise your vibration. If meditation ain't your thing, no sweat. Be sure to find something else that is your thing.

One of my most popular workshops is called VIBE: *Radically Reboot Your Life*. In this workshop, we explore different lifestyle choices that either raise or lower your vibration. If you are interested in learning more about the workshop, you can visit my website at www.shineakron.com/vibe. You can also check out the graphic on page 87.

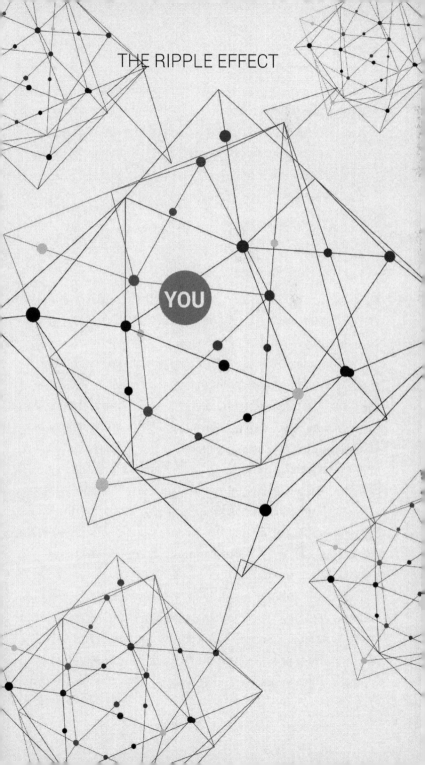

THE RIPPLE EFFECT

YOU

Coming from ego

When first beginning to practice Reiki, one of the biggest pitfalls is coming from a place of ego. We ALL do it – especially when we are working with a person we are close to, someone we love, someone we are trying extra-super-hard to heal. I will explain, but first let me share two basic principles of Reiki.

1. Reiki has its own intelligence (remember, Rei meaning Source or higher-consciousness).

2. Reiki *never* depletes your energy because it is channeled healing. The Reiki practitioner's energies are never used and therefore never depleted.

Here's a HUGE and highlighter-worthy truth: If you feel depleted or not well after giving a Reiki treatment, then you are coming from a place of ego, not a place of Reiki.

What I mean by 'coming from a place of ego' is, whether you know it or not, you are trying to affect a healing. Reiki doesn't work like that. *You* are not doing anything. You are the cord through which the energy flows. To avoid 'coming from a place of ego,' your best bet is to get feeling really good, remain relaxed, and don't give any thought as to whether it's *working* or not. In fact, try not to give any thought to anything.

I commonly find myself having this conversation about *ego* over-and-over again with Reiki practitioners when I'm at events. For that reason, I am going to share a real-life example to bring home the point.

I was approached recently at a yoga event by a level one Reiki practitioner (I will talk in detail about the three different levels of Reiki in Chapter 3 but, for now, understand that level one – in my opinion – means that you have been attuned to the Reiki energy but are still getting comfortable with it while practicing on yourself and maybe others such as family and friends). This level one practitioner began the conversation by saying that she had been providing Reiki to her sister, an on-again-off-again recovering drug addict, and that after practicing on her, she would feel very drained and unwell. Because she felt very drained and unwell after, she felt this meant that she gave-it-her-all during the session. She went on to say how much she loved her sister and how she desperately wanted to help her. Through conversations that she had with others, she came to believe that the reason why she didn't feel well was because the energy that was flowing through her was extra powerful because it was obvious that her sister needed more Reiki than most due to her circumstances.

At the risk of being redundant I am going to break this conversation down, because I think it's *that* important. Also, please forgive my bluntness, again – because I think it's *that* important.

She knows too much. This lovely woman knows too much about her sister, for this particular situation. Sometimes, it is better to know little-to-nothing about the person that you are treating with Reiki. The more unattached you are to the person and her illness, the more unattached you will be to the outcome. When you are attached to the outcome, then you are coming from ego. Let me say that again, when you are attached to the outcome – in any way – then you are coming from ego. And when you are coming from ego, you are not coming from Reiki. It's a distinction worth grasping.

So, now you might say something to me like, but that is the whole reason I became attuned to Reiki because I want to help heal my son, or my husband, or my mom, or my sister... Yes, I get that. If that is the case, then you need to fully understand the rest of what I am about to say before practicing on someone where the outcome is of great importance to you.

She's focusing on the 'drug addict' not her sister's true spirit. Earlier in this chapter, I talked about the traits of a true healer, and how the most important trait of a healer is to hold the space of wellness for another. You simply cannot focus on the problem and expect to feel good after the session. Simple enough. The most important job of a Reiki practitioner is to hold the space of wellbeing for another. If you know the intimate details of their illness/problem, it's harder to do this, but it is possible. This is a good time to get centered with Gassho meditation. If you can't, you need to refer your family member or friend to another Reiki practitioner. You can, of course, still give them your love, your support, and your prayers; but I wouldn't call it Reiki.

Don't give it your all — in fact, just the opposite. She was certainly right about one thing: she was feeling drained and unwell because she 'gave-it-her-all.' However, this is the complete opposite of what you should be doing. Reiki is a channeled energy. You should be allowing the energy to flow through you; and in doing so, you receive the full benefits of Reiki as you are giving it to another – which will never leave you feeling drained or unwell.

You are not here to help anyone. I hear this a lot: "I want to help others." It seems harmless enough. Coming from a lens of helping often comes from ego. Some might say it's just semantics. I would encourage you to look at your intentions when you set out to *help* someone. Seeing someone as needing help, sees them as weak. Seeing someone as needing to be fixed, sees them as broken. *None* of us are weak or broken. We are all whole and perfect. Consider approaching your practice from the lens of service. It's a subtle difference. From my experience, helping and fixing is draining; serving is renewing and fulfilling.

'Unwell' people don't need extra powerful Reiki to heal. There are not different *strengths* of Reiki. I don't care if you are practicing on Hitler or Mother Teresa – a sinner or a saint – someone who is on their death bed or someone who is vibrating at 72 MHz – it just doesn't matter. Reiki makes no distinctions. It sees all life through the eyes of Source. It is both powerful and gentle at the same time. Reiki isn't thinking, "This person is super sick, so we better zap them with extra powerful healing today." It doesn't work like that. Regardless of the person you are sharing Reiki with, Reiki flows in the same powerful, yet gentle way each and every time.

I'll end this section on ego by saying that often you are able to allow the Reiki energy to flow through you unaltered when you work with strangers. This is more difficult when working with family and friends. I know this from years of experience with myself and my students. After Reiki level two training, I give my students the opportunity to practice with 'strangers' during my yoga/Reiki workshops. This is typically the first time they are practicing Reiki on someone other than their family members or friends. Repeatedly, I hear from my students how different the experience is when working with participants in the yoga workshop. For the first time, they can experience Reiki *as intended*, with no ego attached. It's a beautiful thing that I am truly unable to put into words. Once you've *experienced* it, you will know the distinction between coming from ego and allowing Reiki to flow through you unaltered. It's this unaltered state that you are reaching for. This is where miracles happen.

My process

Students often ask me what I'm *thinking* about during a one-on-one Reiki session with another. It's similar to meditating, except, instead of following your breath or using a mantra, your focus is on the Reiki consciousness. This will look different for each person depending on their training and their beliefs. My experience of the Reiki consciousness is one of unconditional love, peace, and wellbeing. Of course, as with other meditations, your mind will wander. If during a session, I start thinking about what I'm going to cook for dinner and how I need to go pick up a tub of sour cream for Taco Tuesday, then, I gently bring my awareness back. Back to the present moment, back to Reiki. At the beginning of a student's practice, these kinds of thoughts are bound to happen more regularly.

It might help to know that, as you provide Reiki to another, you will be receiving deep healing for yourself. I can't emphasize this enough. After *giving* a Reiki session, I feel more alive, more well, more connected than any other time in my life. I think it's because of my process and what is happening as I drift into this deep meditative state during a Reiki session. (I talk more about the benefits of this meditative state in Chapter 5.)

I humbly share with you the process that I have come to use. Early on in my practice, I realized something beautiful. I started to understand what is meant in yoga when we say "namaste" or when we talk about how we are all connected. Before having this realization, I intellectually understood the concept, but I did not fully grasp it until a few years into my

Reiki practice.

My realization came when my husband, Brian, was laying on the Reiki table during a session. It suddenly *occurred* to me that while I was giving him Reiki, it was no longer *my husband* lying there. (What?!) The rendezvous between us was so much deeper than that. In that moment, I realized that *my* higher-self (what I refer to as the 'big me') was having a beautiful conversation with *his* higher-self (the 'big Brian'). Our little selves – the ones made of flesh and blood – were *not* the ones entangled during this fateful Reiki session. It was the closest I've ever felt to my husband (who I've been married to for 20 years). It was a deeper level of intimacy that I can only explain in this way. Instead of my husband laying on the Reiki table, it was a beautiful, amazing soul. A soul that I had the honor of co-creating with on a much deeper level than this physical plain could ever allow. From that moment forward, I began to see my Reiki sessions as a *divine conversation* between my higher-self and the higher-self of my client. When you are co-creating on this level, you know, from the feeling, that ego is *nowhere* to be found. It's like two stars dancing in the night sky; free of any mental and physical boundaries.

PART 2

Let's Graph This Out

I am a visual communication designer, so I couldn't create a book without a few visuals. Right?! Thanks for indulging me.

CHAPTER 3

In a world where instant gratification is king, one might unknowingly cheat themselves of the value each level has to offer when rushing through the journey.

The three levels

There are typically three or four levels of Reiki training offered to students. I teach three. Depending on the Reiki Master, training could look different based on the way the teacher breaks it out. After almost a decade of teaching, I found the following to be the most advantageous way for my students to reap the full benefits of each level. In a world where instant gratification is king, one might unknowingly cheat themselves of the value each level has to offer when rushing through the journey.

I offer this up for consideration by both future and current Reiki students and by Reiki Master teachers. For future and current students, I present this for informational purposes, so you can get an idea of what *could* be taught at each level. Again, keep in mind, depending on the teacher you select for your training, it could look different. For new Reiki Master teachers, I present it for your consideration as an option for how to structure the classes offered to your students. I unassumingly share it, not as the 'correct' or 'perfect' way to teach, but as an option for you to consider.

Level one training

The focus of level one training is Heal Yourself. After you have successfully achieved this level, aside from practicing on family and friends, you are not yet prepared to offer your services to paying clients. Once you're attuned to Reiki in level one, you have immediate access to it. The only thing necessary to begin the flow of Reiki is your intention for it to flow. Your job now is to become comfortable with *this flow*. You do this by practicing on yourself, family and friends; animals and pets are good options too. Until you have the necessary practice, you are not ready for the techniques and symbols that are offered in Reiki level two training.

After Reiki one training, you are encouraged to practice on yourself daily so that you can become comfortable with the Reiki energy. But, I'll let you in on a little secret, another reason to practice on yourself before embarking on Reiki two training is to give you the self-care you need before transitioning to working with clients. As I mention in Chapter 2, self-care is immensely important for Reiki practitioners.

A lot of what is shared in this book is taught in my Reiki one class. Of course, you aren't receiving the attunement here and therefore would not be considered a Reiki practitioner. However, you now have a deeper understanding of what it means to be a Reiki practitioner.

1 HEAL YOURSELF

RECEIVE: Reiki ONE Attunement

LEARN:
✓ What is Reiki, what is a healer
✓ Hand-position to treat yourself, family members and friends

AFTER CLASS:
Goal: Become comfortable with the Reiki energy
Homework: Practice on yourself, family, friends, pets

PREREQUISITE

1 month

2 HEAL OTHERS

RECEIVE: Reiki TWO Attunement

LEARN:
✓ 3 symbols
✓ Techniques to incorporate into your Reiki practice
✓ How to give a full Reiki treatment to a client

AFTER CLASS:
Goal: Skills and knowledge to start your own Reiki practice
Homework: Learn symbols and practice on clients

6 to 12 months

3 TRAIN OTHERS

RECEIVE: MASTER Attunement

LEARN:
✓ 3 symbols
✓ Different healing modalities to incorporate with Reiki
✓ Teaching through student presentations

AFTER CLASS:
Goal: Skills and knowledge to teach your own students
Homework: Learn symbols and attunements

Level two training

The focus of level two training is Heal Others. During this class, there is a lot of information given regarding starting a Reiki practice. The class explores techniques to incorporate into your sessions, how to give a full Reiki treatment, and setting boundaries as you prepare to serve others. Also, this is the first time you are introduced to and attuned to Reiki symbols. This is where things start getting really good. This is my favorite class to teach. And students seem most eager about diving into the next phase of their training.

After taking Reiki two training, I require waiting six to twelve months before taking Master training. This is when the need for instant gratification might kick in. You are super excited about what you've learned and can't wait to learn and experience more. You might even feel an urgency to add the title 'Reiki Master' to your name. Trust me on this one, you need the practice and the experience before taking it to the next level. It probably seems obvious that teaching others should come after you have the necessary practice and experience, but what might not be as obvious is what is happening to you internally. Reiki works in magical ways. It will open up new levels of insight and transformation within and around you. Rushing on to the next level too quickly is a great disservice to yourself; potentially missing the insights that comes with time and sincere reflection.

Master training

The focus of Master training is Teach Others. As a Reiki Master you can teach and attune others to Reiki. Also, the student is attuned to three more symbols. Becoming a Reiki Master, however, is not only about teaching and attuning others to the Reiki energy. It is a life-long journey and lifestyle that one feels compelled toward. It's important to note that the Japanese name for the Master training is Shinpiden, which means mystery teaching. For that reason, understand that the word 'Master' when used in this training does not mean a spiritual master who is completely purified and free from ego. Instead it symbolizes a student's commitment to continually evolve. Some say it's where the final bit of Reiki's *mystery* is transferred to you. However, no matter how much we experience a spiritual awakening, there is always more - a next step, another doorway, a deeper level. This desire for growth and transformation is what ultimately leads people to becoming a Reiki Master. Maybe this is what lead you to this very book; the urge to continually evolve.

I mentioned at the beginning of this chapter that often there are three or four levels of Reiki training. I would like to briefly explain this variation now. In present day, often this Master training is broken out into two parts (levels three and four) which are sometimes referred to as ART (Advanced Reiki Training) and Master Training. It was not always like this. According to my research, ART was born out of the desire for some students to have access to the Usui Master symbol even if they were not ready or interested in being initiated as a Master. Takata, who is known for bringing Reiki to the West, only offered three levels. It is thought that after her passing, some began to break out the Master level into two parts to accommodate different student's needs and desires. As for me, I teach it as one level, as it was initially intended.

Reiki attunements: The healing crisis

I briefly mentioned attunements in Chapter 1. Now, I would like to introduce the concept of what is known as the healing crisis in Reiki.

As a reminder, Reiki attunements connect a Reiki student to the Reiki energy. Reiki is transferred during an attunement process from an experienced Reiki Master to a student. The Reiki attunements can start a cleansing process, referred to as *the healing crisis*, that affects the physical body as well as the mind and emotions. Toxins that have been stored in the body may be released along with feelings and thought patterns that are no longer useful to the Reiki student.

Let me stop here for a moment to explore what I just said. *Stuff* is about to get released. Stuff that has been stored in your body, maybe for years, if not decades, is going to be *freed* due to this attunement. This stuff may include feelings, past traumas, and negative belief systems that you have been holding on to that no longer serve you! Reiki, this divine intelligence, knows exactly what to release to serve you in your journey so that you can become this beautiful, magnificent soul that you were always meant to be. This stuff may have once protected you and you may have once needed it, but often we hang on to it long after its expiration date. And now, through the attunement process, we begin to let it go, and we heal. How freakin' amazing is that?

So, here's where the healing crisis comes in. For a moment, think about what is about to go down. We've been carrying this stuff around with us – stored in us – some of it more painful than others – and now we are about to release it! Wow! Whenever change takes place, even if it is good, a period of adjustment is necessary so that the body and various parts of your life can settle into the healthy conditioning.

The example that I share with my students is similar to that of a detox diet. I'll use the Whole 30 diet as the example. For those of you who aren't familiar with it, here's the gist. Basically, for 30 days, you are allowed to eat unprocessed meat, most nuts, eggs, vegetables (even potatoes) and fruit in moderation. You cannot have sugar, dairy, grains, processed foods, or alcohol of any kind. I'm sure I am missing something (sorry), but you get the point. Now, this sounds like something good to do for your body, right? Especially if you are eating a lot of processed foods filled with chemicals. What some people don't expect when first beginning this diet is that for the first few weeks of eliminating these forbidden foods, you typically feel awful. It's happening because you are cleansing; you are releasing toxins from your body. It takes a week or two for you to start feeling normal. After a short bit of time you feel amazing. This is what's happening after a Reiki attunement too.

I tell you this, not to scare you about the attunement process, but instead, so that you know what's happening when it happens. The last thing I would want you to think is, "Boy, why do I feel so crappy after my Reiki training? I thought this was going to be a good thing." Indeed, it is a good thing! You can't even imagine the blessings that are in store for you.

Some of my students don't notice the cleansing process at all; instead they feel amazing and full of energy in the days and weeks to follow an attunement. I'll give you an idea of how it *might* affect you. Typically, the farther out of alignment you are, the more you will notice the cleansing process. Let's go back to our Whole 30 example. If you are eating McDonalds and drinking your fair share of martinis on a Saturday night (no judgment here!), then you are going to have a harder go-at-it than someone who eats roasted lemon chicken with steamed organic vegetables and passes on the martinis. The same is true for the attunement. If you are caring for yourself regularly, - maybe you have a meditation or yoga practice (which both release toxins) - then for you, the adjustments may be minimal.

Here's what's so beautiful: attunements affect everyone differently because we are all unique. Reiki, knowing your uniqueness, will make the perfect alterations so that you can become the best version of you. This is the promise of Reiki.

So, here's what you should do if/when you start to feel the healing crisis after an attunement. Notice and let it be. Allow it to come up and release. Give yourself what you need during this time. If it is more sleep, indulge in more sleep. If it is meditation and contemplation, do that. Maybe you just want to binge watch *This is Us* and have a cry fest for one weekend. That's perfectly alright too. My yoga teacher once told me, crying only means one thing. It means you are releasing resistance. And that's a good thing.

Reiki symbols

Reiki symbols are sacred. It is part of the Reiki tradition to keep them confidential. Unless speaking with a Reiki two practitioner or Reiki Master, you are asked not to discuss the specifics of the symbols. For that reason, I will not share the names or the pictures of the symbols in this book. Instead, I will share that Reiki symbols are one of the most powerful aspects of a Reiki practice. Reiki symbols are like keys that open doors to higher levels of awareness and manifestation. The power of the symbols is not in their outward appearance. Instead, the power and the effectiveness of the symbols comes

from the Reiki attunement that is given during the Reiki training. To learn more about the symbols, you'll just have to wait
for Reiki two training. (I'm excited for you to find out!)

CHAPTER 4

*Illness and pain, whether physical or mental, are
only the manifestation...*

The four levels

As a Reiki Master, one of the most important things that I can share with my students and clients is this concept of healing on four levels. If you want to see any lasting change, you must consider each of the four levels; focusing on one or two usually is not enough. The first step is to learn about the four different levels as seen in the graphic on the following page.

Let me start off by saying, yes, Reiki is amazing, and I've seen miracles unfold before my eyes more than once. Reiki – among other things – can open up pathways in your energetic body that are blocked. It leaves you high-flying for hours, maybe even days, and symptoms vanish. And then bam! A day, a week, or a month later, you are right back to where you started before the treatment. It's not so different than anything else that we might attempt to do to 'make us feel better' such as

Physical
The language of the physical is chemistry; atoms and molecules

HEAL WITH:
Diet, exercise, rest, vitamins, herbs, medical doctors

Emotional
The language of the emotional is imagery

HEAL WITH:
Visualization, imagination, meditation

Mental
The language of the mental is words, thoughts, beliefs

HEAL WITH:
Affirmations, therapists, forgiveness, meditatio

Spiritual
The language of the spiritual is energy

HEAL WITH:
The identity beyond your ego: Reiki, chakras and other alternative healing techniques and modalities

Heal
ON FOUR LEVELS

acupuncture, yoga, or a prescription from our doctor. Have you ever noticed how you have this nagging thing that happens to you over and over again? It keeps showing up no matter what healer you see, pill you take, diet you start, book you read, or doctor you consult! Why?

I've already told you the answer, but some of us don't want to hear it. The reason we don't want to hear it is because it seems like a lot of work to focus on *four* different levels. I know, I hear ya. I only take a shower a few times a week, and that's if I'm lucky. (Ok, I'm lying - at this point, it has nothing to do with luck, it's more that I just don't care, ha!) Our time is precious, and it seems like a lot of work to focus on FOUR things. Some people have even challenged me by saying it is much *easier* and more effective to take a pill and be done with it. But, I know you - my wellness warrior – would never think like that. So, let's explore each of the four levels here.

Physical

The language of the physical is chemistry – atoms and molecules. If we want to heal on this level, we work with diet/ nutrition, exercise, rest, vitamins, medical doctors, and quitting bad habits such as smoking and drinking. This is where a majority of human beings focus most of their time. It makes sense. This is the level that is most tangible. In fact, most people are probably only aware of this level; they don't even consider the other three a 'thing.' You don't need me to tell you that a person can be in optimal physical health and still be in need of healing.

Emotional

The language of emotion is imagery. If we want to heal on

this level, we can work with visualization, our imagination, and meditation. For example, meditating on the idea that you are already healed.

Mental

The language of the mental is words, thoughts, ideas, and beliefs. This is a BIG one! I mean, who doesn't have a negative stream running through their mind from time-to-time. If we want to heal on this level, we can work with affirmations, therapists, counselors, and even forgiveness.

The late Louise Hay authored a book about working with affirmations called *Heal Your Body*. This book reads like a giant chart. On the left side, it gives the physical ailment. In the middle, it gives the negative belief that is causing the physical ailment. On the right, the book suggests an affirmation that one might use to change the wiring of the brain from a negative belief, that no longer serves, to a positive belief that enriches and even heals. This is an example of how one might begin to heal on the mental level. This book has been a great resource to me, especially when working with clients and students who want to go deeper.

Spiritual

The last and final level brings us back full-circle. The language of the spirit is energy. If we want to heal on this level, we work with the identity beyond the ego. There are many different energy techniques, such as Reiki, that aid in healing on this level. They are powerful, and miracles can happen.

The good and the bad news

Now for the good and the bad news. Since I'm a glass-half-full-kind-of-girl, let's go with the good news first. The good news is healing is in your hands. You can make the choices and put in the love necessary to *heal yourself* on all four levels.

Now, the bad news – healing is in your hands. (I know, it is the same news – tricky huh?) And, let's face it, sometimes we would rather give our power away, whether that's to a doctor, a healer, a pill, or a fill-in-the-blank, instead of empowering ourselves.

Illness and pain, whether physical or mental, are only the manifestation. Sometimes it is beneficial to see the illness and the pain as a portal; the manifestation can be meaningful and brilliantly intelligent in waking us up. Maybe you are there right now. Maybe you are waking up to your manifestations and realizing that there must be more to these symptoms. After all, some say that our cells regenerate daily/weekly and we have a whole new body every seven years. So why do we continue to have the same chronic issues, and in some cases, for our entire lives? Perhaps it's because we continue to *regurgitate* the same negative habits over and over again which brings us the same results.

Let me give you an example of what it would look like to heal on four levels. I once knew a woman. She was young, in her early thirties. She had a great job, a beautiful family, a wonderful life, but she was plagued with severe anxiety. There were days when she suffered from such sever panic attacks that she couldn't leave her home or get out of the car to go into the grocery store with her husband and her son. At its worst, sometimes when driving, she thought about what it would be like to not hit the brakes and slam right into the car in front of her. She thought that would be easier. The doctors wanted to put her on antidepressants, but she wanted to find the root of her anxiety. She visited a naturopathic doctor who performed some tests on her. One of the things the doctor found out during the tests is that this woman's hormones were nine times the level of a normal woman. *Nine times.* This woman could tell the severity of the issue by the way the doctor looked at her when she said, "I don't know how anyone could deal with levels this high." (Imagine how you feel during certain times of the month when your hormones are only slightly out of natural balance.) The doctor explained that one of the reasons why her hormones were so high is because the tests also indicated that she was highly sensitive to dairy. When I first heard this story, I thought that seemed weird, why would her hormones be nine times the normal level because she was eating dairy. Apparently, as the doctor explained, her liver was working over-time to clear the toxins from the food. This meant that her liver wasn't able to effectively clear her hormones from her system each month. Obviously, the doctor suggested that she stop eating dairy and come back in six months to be retested. She did as the doctor said and returned in six months to be retested. To the *surprise* of everyone, after six months, her hormone levels were in normal range. Apparently, it was unheard of for hormone levels to drop so drastically in such a short period of time. The doctor had hoped to see progress but never expected to see normal levels. What the doctor didn't take into consideration is that this woman was not only healing on the physical level by changing her diet, but this woman was also healing on the other three levels (emotionally, mentally, and spiritually). She was practicing yoga on a regular basis, using affirmations, doing guided meditations, and she had even been attuned to Reiki and was practicing on herself daily. I know the intimate details of this story. I know how desperate she felt. I know how determined she was to feel normal and how important it was to be well, so she could take care of her son without the help of others. I know the urgency she felt to heal. I know she would have done anything necessary. I know...because this woman used to be me. Ultimately, I know how it feels to claim back a life that was once lost. And I know it requires the healing of all four levels.

This chapter gives you the chance to *reexamine* your definition of healing; your definition of wellbeing. This concept is the missing piece in most of our practices; in most of our lives. It is the piece that can bring about lasting change – once and for all. Keep reading. With each remaining chapter, this concept will become increasingly clear.

CHAPTER 5

Those with a sincere heart, will one-day look back at their old life and see it as unrecognizable.

Advantages of Reiki training

Being able to provide healing for yourself is one of the obvious advantages of becoming a Reiki practitioner. What surprises and delights Reiki students the most are the advantages that aren't so obvious; the ones students start to experience months and years after their first attunement when Reiki becomes a *way of life*. Here are some benefits to consider and cultivate along your journey.

Vibration

Attract higher quality experiences. This one is simple. Reiki raises your vibration. Your vibration attracts *life* to you; people, places, things, and experiences. Once you begin to raise your vibration through Reiki, you will begin to attract higher quality experiences into your life. In fact, those with a sincere heart, will one-day look back at their old life and see it as unrecognizable.

Wellbeing

Live in a place of peace, love, and joy. Living in peace, love, and joy is our natural state. But, as we move along our physical paths, we pick up a lot of *stuff* that keeps us from seeing or feeling this natural state. Reiki, through the attunement process, starts a cleansing process and we begin to release the resistance that is stored in our physical bodies. Once released, we begin to see glimpses of our natural state. Eventually, these glimpses turn into minutes, hours, and sometimes days. Peace, love, and joy. Peace, love and joy. Peace, love, and joy. Over and over again.

Meditate

Experience deeper levels of consciousness. One of the greatest gifts of *giving* Reiki to another is the ability to access deeper levels of consciousness, with practice of course. Reiki is a seamless flow with infinite intelligence. From my experience, the higher conversation that I speak of in Chapter 2 allows me to drop into a deep meditative state: one that I cannot normally access in meditation. Often, my mind-chatter will come to a complete halt when I'm with a client. Can you even imagine the health benefits of this? I assure you, I am flying high for hours, sometimes even days after giving Reiki to another. It's amazing. My wish is for everyone to experience it at least one time in her life. That's what I call getting high!

Empowerment

Take charge of your own health and life. First and foremost, I am a teacher of empowerment. I love seeing people take charge of their own health and life. Reiki gives you the avenue to do this. It doesn't mean you don't go to the doctor or take

ADVANTAGES OF REIKI TRAINING

Vibration
Attract higher quality experiences

Wellbeing
Live in a place of peace, love and joy

Meditate
Experience deeper levels of consciousness

Empowerment
Take charge of your own health and life

Evolve
Grow into your personal mission

Heal
Serve others in their journey

medication when needed (if that feels right to you). Instead, it means that you don't *solely* rely on doctors, healers, and medicine for your health. You become proactive and take care of yourself before the illness or the disease manifests physically. It's a subtle difference. I don't know about you, but my goal is to avoid being on 20 different prescriptions in the latter part of my life. Instead, I want to manage my health through consistent healthy lifestyle choices; the prime one being Reiki.

Evolve

Grow into your personal mission. At the beginning of every Reiki training class, I ask the students what their intentions are for learning Reiki. You know, a why-are-you-here kind of question. No one has ever said to me, "I'm here because I want to grow into my personal mission." But inevitably, that is where it takes them. For most, Reiki is much more unassuming. Normally, people are looking for relief from their current situation and they've heard that maybe Reiki can assist. That was my story. Little did I know that Reiki would transform me and my life beyond my wildest dreams. I've *intentionally* left the talk of religion out of this book, because Reiki is *not* a religion. Reiki is, however, a spiritual practice. Reiki is the way the Divine worked through me to support me in fulfilling *my* personal mission. And I am so grateful.

Heal

Serve others in their journey. Early in my practice, a friend came to me for Reiki two to three days after each of his chemo sessions while being treated for brain cancer. It's been awhile, but I think it amounted to 12 sessions in total. He only missed one. He became very sick after missing that one session. It's not a coincidence. As the chemo fought the cancer, he needed something to restore balance back into his body. That something was Reiki. He was grateful not only for the Reiki, but also for the chemo. He's still cancer free after all these years. I'm blessed to have served, however small the role, in his journey.

Giving Reiki is exponentially more powerful than receiving it from another. Stop for a moment and consider what is happening when you *give* Reiki. At that moment when you lay hands on another, with the intention of giving Reiki, you have direct access to the energy that creates worlds. This energy is flowing through you. (Honestly, you always have access to this energy whether or not you are attuned to Reiki. Reiki, however, provides the focused way in which you sync up with this energy.)

Imagine, for a moment, that the Divine takes form as a man in the physical. He breaths; he has a body, two legs, and a pair of lips; he walks; and he talks. You can actually see him, touch him, and talk to him. He is all powerful and all knowing. He created you and he created this world and everything in it. He has infinite wisdom and infinite power. What if you were able to meet with him? Maybe you share a meal, maybe you take a walk in nature, maybe he visits you at your home and he sits with you on the couch. As you sit there with him, you feel his unconditional love. It literally envelopes you and you feel warm and safe; fully supported. Sitting that close to him on the couch, you know - maybe for the first time in your entire life - that everything is ok. Even better than ok. It's perfect. You don't know why you know this, but you do. In the blink of an eye, everything makes sense. Everything that seemed confusing or frustrating before, now seems right. Maybe you even chuckle to yourself because you see how silly it seems now to have worried or fussed about anything. Maybe while sitting on the couch, you start to have a conversation with him. Maybe during that conversation, he shares with you the secrets of the universe. The two of you marvel in its magnificence. And right before he leaves, he bestows upon you the energy necessary to heal yourself and others. Or maybe you realize in this moment, that healing isn't even necessary. You see with clarity for the first time; you see the wholeness and perfection of this world and everything in it.

Now, what if I told you that everything that you just experienced while sitting on this couch is what happens when the Reiki energy flows through you. When you give Reiki, you are presented with a glimpse of what it would be like to hang out with the Divine.

Does that scare you? Does it make you feel uncomfortable to consider yourself in this light? Do you feel not worthy, or not good enough, or too small and inconsequential for this to be true? Is it possible that this is available to you in every moment and you still choose the darkness over the light? Maybe it's time. It's time for you to shine your light.

PART 3

Rapid-fire Practical Advice on Hot Topics

Hang on tight, it's about to go down...

CHAPTER **6**

Transactions involving money, above all else, are an exchange of energy.

Money

New Reiki practitioners often come to me, when first starting a public practice, to ask for advice about what (and if) to charge for their services. On the surface, this chapter might be about money, but go deeper and it's about our own *worthiness*. Therefore, this chapter, this advice, is relevant to our entire lives.

- Reiki is energy.
- Money is energy.
- One is not inherently more spiritual than the other.
- Really, I promise.
- Transactions involving money, above all else, are an exchange of energy.
- Transactions, whether spiritual in nature or not, crave balance.

- All interactions and relationships are intended to be two-sided and in balance.
- Some suggest pricing your Reiki session to match that of a massage in your area.
- I suggest you charge what makes you feel at peace.
- Those who pay for a session are not paying for the Reiki energy itself. Rather, they are paying for the time and effort you have put forth to learn Reiki and the time that you spend away from your family and other obligations.
- Time, after all, is a resource that we cherish the most.
- Considering this, you are the only one who can determine if charging $20, $50, or $100 feels right for you.
- The question of worthiness should NEVER be part of this equation.
- Know that you are worthy.
- Know that your clients are going to benefit from you greatly.
- Know that they are attracted to you for a reason.
- The manifestation of money is evidence of your *personal alignment.*
- Takata, the person responsible for brining Reiki to the United States, believed that people put more value on items and services if they pay for them.
- In fact, she charged $10,000 for her Reiki Master training almost 50 years ago (which is like charging $333,526.46 today!!!).
- Imagine for a moment that you paid $30,000 for a brand-new shiny car.
- Now imagine if the same car was given to you for *free.*
- Which car would you *value* more?

- Some practitioners I know charge $40 for a session. I charge $60. There is no right or wrong amount.
- The only way to mess it up is to charge an amount that you aren't comfortable with charging.
- Lastly, focus less on what to charge and more on the *value* you are adding.

Let us be silent, so that we may hear the whisper of God.

RALPH WALDO EMERSON

Intuition

Intuition is one of the greatest assets you have for both cultivating wellness and becoming a great Reiki practitioner. Here's some advice for strengthening your intuition.

- Ask for it! This may seem silly, but the simple act of saying to yourself, "hey, I am ready for guidance, bring it on," is enough to kick-start that relationship with the 'big-you' that I speak of in Chapter 2.
- Once you ask for it, you must honor it by following your impulses.
- At first, you are going to be unsure if it's your inner-guidance or just some weird thought popping into your mind. You need to get used to following the impulse.
- Each time you follow the impulse and it's validated, you get

more and more confidence, which increases the quality and quantity of the guidance received.

- Give gratitude for the guidance you receive.
- There have been times when I've dropped to my knees in gratitude for that which I've received. You should too.
- Be patient with it.
- Ugh, I know, patience is a virtual but trust me, it's worth it.
- Expect it. Start to believe it. Own it.
- Quiet the mind often.
- If you aren't ever quieting your mind, how-the-heck can you expect to hear the gentle whisper inside?
- Start meditating – for reals! (Just about every spiritual guru you love and know does it.)
- Eventually, after quieting the mind often, it will be less of a whisper and more like a knowing.
- Gassho meditation, the first pillar of Reiki, can help you quiet your mind. (We practiced this in Chapter 2.)

Examples of what intuition *might* look like during a Reiki session:

A feeling in your body that you know isn't related to you (i.e. pain in the shoulder, tingling in the knee etc.). Last week, I was giving a Reiki treatment to a client who had just pulled a muscle in her shoulder, when I laid my hands on her shoulder, I felt tingling in *my* shoulder. I imagine that this tingling is an indication that her cells are renewing. In this case, I knew about her shoulder, but sometimes clients don't share, and that's ok. You need to be centered and quiet enough in your mind to be able to pick up on it, *whether* or not a client has shared it with you. When you receive this intuition, like the tingling in my shoulder, you pause and be with it until you get the nudge to move on.

A thought occurs in the form of a suggestion for your client. The second pillar of Reiki is known as Reiji-ho; it's the process for preparing to give Reiki to another. The last part of this process is to ask for guidance during a Reiki session. If you are sincere in your asking and clear in your mind, you may receive blocks of information that manifest as a thought for you to pass on to your client. Remember we are all connected. Sometimes the suggestion is very specific. Other times, it may be a suggestion to seek out a book, a person, or an experience.

Heat or other noticeable differences in a client's body. While moving the hands along the client's body, you may pick up differences. For me, it shows up as heat or warmth in a certain area. If you notice this, it's your intuition telling you something. With practice, you'll begin to know what it looks like and what it means for you.

A feeling that you want to stay longer in a certain area/with a certain hand-position, even if you don't know why. As far as intuition goes, this is my favorite nudge. I love when I am working on a client and I am in a certain area of the body and I get this feeling to stay. It's *not* a feeling like, "Oh no, something bad is going on here, you better stay." Actually, it's just the opposite. It's a feeling of *contentment*; an undeniable urge to just stay put where you are. Sometimes it's so strong that the room could be on fire around me and I wouldn't even care because I know this is exactly where I need to be. Honor this feeling. Once I had a client tell me, before a session, that she would like for me to focus on her left knee for medical reasons. When I got to her abdomen, however, I didn't want to move. My analytical mind said, "Move along, we need to get to that left knee." But my intuition said, "Don't you dare. This is exactly where you need to be." Later, I learned she was pregnant and having complications. (!)

Story of when I refused to listen to my intuition. This is one of my very favorite stories to share with students about a time when I *refused* to listen to my intuition. A colleague referred a client to me after this person had knee surgery. This was the first time this person had ever had Reiki. When she arrived, we talked briefly about expectations of the session. I explained how I would start at the head and end at the feet. I decided that, even though she was coming specifically for healing of her knee and entire leg, I still wanted to give her a typical 'standard session.' I would, however, spend more time on her knee and leg than a typical session. Quickly, after starting at her head, I began to get this strong nudge that I needed to skip over most of the normal hand positions and work solely on the lower half of her body. I ignored the nudge and continued on with the standard hand positions. Before I explain what happened next, I'll give you a lay-of-the-land in my Reiki room. At the time, I was practicing in a very small room, maybe seven feet by ten feet. It was just big enough for me to fit a Reiki table with enough room for me to maneuver around it on all sides. I had a couple of laminated posters on the walls. One was a reflexology poster and the second was a master chart of 908 asanas by Dharma Mittra. Both posters were held in place with tacks. I finally reached the client's right knee and *the moment* I placed my hands on her knee, two tacks shot out of the wall as if they were bullets out of a gun. It startled me, to say the least.

I instantly started laughing (in my head, of course) because I finally got the message. It said loud and clear, *this* is where you need to be! It was a great reminder to always listen to my intuition. After the session concluded, I said to the client, "Please be careful when you get off the Reiki table. There were two tacks that came out of the wall and I don't want you to step on them." She looked at me and said, "Yeah, I noticed that. It was when you touched my knee." We just smirked at each other because we both had an unspoken reverence for what some might have considered a coincidence.

I'll say it again: we are all connected. The more you practice listening to your intuition, the more obvious it becomes. Intuition allows you to *translate* the energy of others through the senses. And the translation will be unique to you. (More on this in Chapter 12.)

CHAPTER 8

Reiki facilitates the flow of our life-force energy, which is made evident by the opening of our chakras.

Chakras

Chakras are the body's energetic system. They are most commonly talked about as seven in number. Chakras correspond to massive nerve centers in the physical body; they also tell a story about our mental, emotional, and spiritual states. There are thousands and thousands of books, internet pages, and classes dedicated to learning more about this ancient Indian concept. Here, I am not so much trying to explain what chakras are, but instead, describing how I've incorporated them into my interactions with clients.

- Before a Reiki session, I test the seven chakras of a client in order to guide the session.
- Chakras start at the base of your spine and follow the spine through the crown of your head (see graphic on next page).

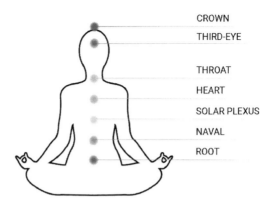

CROWN
THIRD-EYE

THROAT
HEART
SOLAR PLEXUS
NAVAL
ROOT

- Each chakra represents something different.*
- Chakra is a Sanskrit word that means wheel or vortex. That's important to know because...
- Chakras can be observed using a pendulum.
- With practice and alignment, a pendulum can pick up on the energy wheel of the chakra.
- From my experience, the pendulum will swing either clockwise or counterclockwise.
- Clockwise means open.
- Counterclockwise means closed.
- When a chakra is closed, it means the energy is blocked; the ki is not flowing in an optimal way.
- A chakra can be closed for physical, emotional, mental, or spiritual reasons.
- After testing thousands of chakras, I've noticed that, on average, people typically have one to four chakras closed (out of seven).
- I share this statistic with clients that I am testing.
- I share it so that no one becomes alarmed.

- There's no need for alarm.
- I am hyper aware, when I am testing a person's chakras, that this could be the first time she has ever received this type of evaluation. Therefore, letting her know that it's typical for one to four chakras to be closed, can ease her mind.
- After tracking chakra tests with my clients over the years, I've surmised that chakras can be closed either chronically, or for a-moment-in-time.
- Chronically closed means that a particular chakra is closed each and every (or almost every) time I test the client at the beginning of a session.
- Normally, the chakra is chronically closed because the client has a chronic habit keeping it closed.
- It seems obvious when I say it out loud. Doesn't it?
- The chronic habit can be physical, emotional, mental, or spiritual in nature. (Remember the levels I spoke of in Chapter 4?)
- Sometimes, I observe the chakra closed for a-moment-in-time reason.
- Moment-in-time means something is going on, *right now* in the client's life, that has caused the energy to be blocked.
- A simple example is the throat chakra could be observed closed on a client who has a sore throat.
- A more serious example is the closing of the heart chakra because the client has just lost a pet.
- In this example, the heart chakra might stay closed for a longer period of time than the sore throat example. Both are still a moment-in-time examples.

- There *are* those few who consistently have all seven chakras open.
- In fact, I observe this less than five-percent of the time.
- It is not something that happens by accident.
- I would call these people, wellness warriors.
- They are making consistent lifestyle choices (on all four levels) to increase their vibration.
- Practicing yoga – as you are about to find out in Chapter 11 – is one of the ways you can increase your vibration, and on more than one of the levels that we talked about in Chapter 4.
- Side note here: yoga is one of the magic bullets. If you aren't doing yoga already, know that it is a game-changer.
- But I digress. Back to my story about chakras and yoga.
- I was at a yoga festival as a vendor for my company, SHINE, giving free chakra testings with a colleague. After testing hundreds of people, we noticed a theme.
- On average, yogis at this festival had one to two closed chakras.
- The average was lower than the norm because the practice of yoga offers alignment; it offers balance; it opens up the body, the mind, and the spirit.
- I've also seen extreme cases where all seven chakras are *closed.*
- Ninety-nine times out of 100, this is because the person is in the process of extreme healing.
- For example, I have had several clients who have come to me after their chemo sessions, and all chakras are observed as closed.

- I have also had clients come to me after chemo sessions and *not* all of their chakras were closed.
- Know this!! It's the point of this *entire* chapter.
- Regardless of what I observe at the beginning of a Reiki session, I have never had anyone leave a one-on-one session without all seven chakras open.
- Never.
- They are all open – all seven – every time.
- Does this surprise you?
- Not me.
- That is what Reiki does.
- Reiki facilitates the flow of energy within the body.
- The flow that is vital to our wellbeing.

*If you'd like to learn more about what it means when a particular chakra is closed, you can visit www.shineakron.com/chakrachart to download a free chakra chart.

> If you press your temple and your root chakra at the same time, you can screenshot your soul. 🖤

CHAPTER **9**

I closed my mouth and spoke to you in a hundred silent ways.

RUMI

Practicing on Reiki clients

There is nothing more intimate, more divine, than giving Reiki to another. Tread lightly and never underestimate the *enormity*.

- You are entering sacred space...your family member, friend or client is an expression of the Divine and the space they occupy is sacred ground.
- For this reason, place all outcomes with the Divine.
- Remember, it is not you that is affecting a healing – that's ego. You are there to bask in the energy *with* them.
- Always move into their energy and physical space gently and with love.
- When finished, remove your hands slowly...the two of you are now connected by energy.

- When finished, remove your hands slowly...the two of you are now connected by energy.
- Nope, it's not a typo! I said it *twice* because it's *that* important.
- You are now connected by energy and releasing that energy too quickly can be unpleasant.
- You may have experienced this before.
- Maybe you experienced it in a yoga class when being given a hands-on assist, particularly in savasana.
- It's the same whether or not you are using Reiki.
- If you are touching another person, you are in her energy field. Removing your hands too quickly feels unpleasant for that person.
- Remember who and what we are. We are energy and we are all connected.
- If it is your family member, friend, or client's first Reiki session, explain the process to them.
- One of the best things you can do for a client is create an environment that is conducive to relaxation and releasing resistance.
- If they are nervous or apprehensive about the session because it's their first time, put them at ease by sharing the details of what to expect.
- Never diagnose or tell anyone something is wrong. (More about this in the next chapter when I share an important teachable moment.)
- This is obvious, but worth saying...never *tell* anyone they will be healed by having a Reiki treatment.
- That doesn't mean that I don't think it. That doesn't mean

that it's not my wish for them. But, I don't tell anyone, with certainty, that they will be healed. (I know it's not in my hands, and I know that to completely heal is to heal on four levels; not just the spiritual level.)

CHAPTER 10

The journey of a thousand miles begins with one step.

LAO TZU

For the newbies

At one point in time, we were all 'new.' That's how you start off – new. Often, we want to jump over this newness and be the expert. But boy, there's so much joy in the learning. I hope to always be new at something. That is how I grow; and evolving is the entire point of life. Whether you are new to Reiki or new to this wellness warrior mentality, here's my advice for you.

- Competition is only relevant on the physical plain. Live a life on the spiritual plain where there is *enough* for everyone.
- That might sound like an odd place to start, but it's *everything.*
- If you can get this right, you will do just fine (or better than fine) in *anything* you tackle in life.
- Get clear about the type of clients/people you want to

attract into your practice/life.

- Set your own tone.
- You'd be wise to be intentional about setting the tone for your practice.
- When I first began my practice, I was not intentional. In those days, I was living with severe anxiety.
- That is what brought me to Reiki.
- I bet you can guess the type of client I was attracting.
- It didn't feel good.
- It was too close to home.
- It was a mirror that I was not strong enough to look into.
- These days, I am emotionally, mentally, and spiritually strong.
- My intentions reflect and attract a similar vibration.
- Let your mantra be: I want to co-create with those who want what I have to offer.
- Another good mantra: I want to teach those who are open to what I know.
- When it no longer feels good, stop doing it.
- Whatever it is, stop doing it.
- You can't even begin to imagine what continuing on with something that doesn't feel good does to your point of attraction and your spirit.
- When giving Reiki, the goal is to get out of your head and into your heart.
- You do this by practicing Reiki.
- Practice on yourself, practice on family members and friends, practice on your dog, practice on your cat.
- Reiki your food, your home, and your job.

- Practice, practice, practice.
- Ultimately, words don't teach, experience does.
- In order to truly know Reiki, you must practice it.
- The same goes for any other wellness warrior practice.
- The best way to know yoga is to practice it. You can't truly know yoga by reading about it in a book or attending seminars with a guru.
- The best way to know peace is to practice it. You can't know true peace by sitting in your room meditating (although please do that too). You must be in the world.
- ...even with the people and experiences that are difficult.
- ...especially with the people and experiences that are difficult.
- Remember, above all else, that the greatest gift you can give to another is your presence.
- Be in the moment.
- If you can commit to that, and that alone, everything else will fall into place.

Newbies, here's my personal *teachable moment* that I mentioned in the last chapter:

Tread very lightly when sharing with a client what you experienced during a session, particularly when you are new. When you are new to Reiki and getting comfortable with the energy, you may notice things *shifting* within another's energy and you might not know what it means. For this reason, it's best if you keep that to yourself until you have more experience. Let me explain. Early in my practice, I told a friend that I noticed something weird going on in her abdomen area after the conclusion of a practice session with her. I said it to her recklessly. Later, I found out she was concerned by what I had said (freaked out is more like it) and went to a doctor to try to see what was wrong. Now, years later, I know that when working at the abdomen area it can often kick-start a person's digestion. That is what I *felt* on my friend, her digestion. That's it, just her digestion. I know that now, because I experience it often with clients. At the time, my practice was new, and I didn't know. I opened my mouth and caused concern for another. May you learn from my mistake. This is why practice is the best teacher. If you are unsure about something you notice during your practice and want to talk about it, I'd love to hear. Please email me at cortneyshineakron@outlook.com.

CHAPTER 11

*Life isn't about finding yourself. Life is about
creating yourself.*

GEORGE BERNARD SHAW

Deliberate creation

If I were in the business of convincing people – which I'm not - I would try to convince you of your own power. Said more accurately, I would try to empower you to make changes in your life to move you in the direction of your dreams. Often, I hear people arguing for their own limitations. It's what we do. It's a thing. If you don't believe me, start to observe the conversations of those around you. You'll hear them say things like:

"I wish I could quit my job, but I won't find another job making this much money."

"Cancer runs in my family."

"I don't have a degree."

"I'm just a mom."

"My dad had anxiety and so do I."

"That's just who I am."

"I'm so busy."

"There's not enough time in the day."

"I wish I could."

I could go on. I could fill up an entire book with what people say as they argue for their own limitations. You might even be saying some of these statements to yourself. But they're all just stories. Stories that we tell ourselves. Maybe the story once served a purpose. Maybe even *that* is a story. Regardless, why not start telling a different story? A story that empowers. Remember, we are so free, we can choose our own bondage. And often we do. Maybe sharing my story can *convince* you or at least give you something to think about.

- You are the creator of your world.
- Literally.
- Your personal frequency is ultimately what creates your experiences.
- Moreover, the level of your vibration is what is bringing things into your experience.
- You have access to thoughts, people, and situations based on the level of your vibration.
- Often, we unknowingly create through our observations of the world around us.
- You observe something and that dictates your vibration.
- You observe something good, you feel good, you attract good.
- You observe something bad, you feel bad, you attract bad.
- (BTW – stop watching the news.)
- I use the terms 'good' and 'bad' loosely because nothing is inherently good or bad until we assign meaning to it.
- What if you decided to move your focus from what you are

observing and started to *deliberately* focus on what you want?

- More specifically, what if you stopped focusing on your physical ailment and started to focus on your wellbeing?
- Here is what happened to me.
- As I've mentioned, I first started practicing Reiki because I suffered from anxiety. In fact, I had a dark-night-of-the-soul moment.
- After I started to come out of it, as I began to rise, I was determined to figure out what was *wrong* with me. What was the root of this anxiety?
- What I know now is that the root of the anxiety - in no specific terms - was my vibration and what was manifesting physically was the symptom of that vibration.
- But back to the story.
- I was so determined to find out what was causing my anxiety and to stop it, once and for all.
- Ironically, my incessant focus on finding the cause of my anxiety is what held me in its grip.
- You know, one step forward and two steps back.
- The anxiety was sneaky.
- I'd find a new seminar, book, or teacher that - at first glance - would change my life. I would feel better for a moment and then fall right back into its grips.
- I'd find a new herb, a new essential oil, a new meditation – it would make me feel better, but for how long?
- These things which are high in vibration, no doubt, raised my personal frequency.
- But still, I suffered.

- What kept me in the grips of the anxiety for so long - for much longer than I needed to be - was the mere fact that I continued to focus on the anxiety. More specifically, the cause of the anxiety.
- One day, after receiving my cortisol level results from my naturopathic doctor, I heard a whisper.
- The whisper said, "Your high cortisol levels are not causing your anxiety. Your anxiety is causing your high cortisol levels."
- You might read this and think – duh, Cortney!
- But for me, up until that point, it was never obvious.
- I was so consumed with *what* was causing the anxiety; I never considered that my incessant seeking for an answer was the one thing that *kept* me there.
- And if you know me, you know I'm like a dog-on-a-bone.
- I'm relentless.
- Could I eat something different? Could I meditate more? Should I run in the morning? Maybe I'm not doing enough yoga. I read somewhere Gaba would help...let's try that...if I could just get these damn cortisol levels down, my anxiety would subside.
- That was me, until that fateful whisper.
- Then I realized.
- It's time to let it go.
- It's time to stop trying to find the cause of the anxiety.
- That was the first day of the rest of my life.
- The day that I fell back into my natural state; one where there is always peace and wellbeing.
- At first, after this realization, I had to remind myself to let go.

- I had to retrain the way I had reacted for years.
- I invite you to replace 'anxiety' with what ails you.
- Maybe it's migraines. Maybe it's an auto immune disease. Maybe it's fill-in-the-blank.
- Maybe it's a bad marriage. Maybe it's an unfulfilling job. Maybe it's a lack of money.
- The 'problem' doesn't matter.
- You can shift your focus away from that which is not serving you, to that which you desire.
- Stop searching the internet about your problem. Stop texting your mom about it. Stop talking about it over lunch with a friend. Stop joining groups about it. Stop complaining about it. Stop giving it YOUR POWER.
- Just stop.
- Stop and pivot.
- For me, it was pivoting away from the cause of my anxiety to *peace*.
- It's not only a shift in focus that is necessary, but also a shift in your vibration.
- The external world is only a reflection of your current vibration.*
- Trying to control or influence the external is a futile fight in action.
- I'll leave you with one last thought.
- Right now, someone is living a life of her dreams, all because she examined the limitations she was placing on herself and said, "No more!"
- This can be you.
- It's my greatest wish for you.

*Learn more about the lifestyle choices that raise and lower your vibration in the graphic that follows. This is only a partial list; there are many, many more.

Reiki facilitates the flow of life force energy. It is one of the fastest ways to kick-start one's wellbeing, whether giving or receiving.

The feeling of *Gratitude* is one of the highest frequencies. Starting a consistent gratitude practice is sure to raise not only your vibe but others too.

Yoga also facilitates the flow of life force energy. Its one of the only lifestyle choices that hits each of the four levels from Chapter 4.

If you dont have a *Meditation* practice, this is the most accessible way to raise your vibe because its free and no experience is required. Just sit and be.

The *Food* you eat to fuel your body contributes mightily to your vibe. Fresh, raw foods are of the highest vibe and processed foods are the lowest.

Your vibe attracts your *Tribe*, but the opposite is also true. Start to be aware of the people in your life and notice who is raising or lowering your vibe.

Words & *Thoughts* have frequencies. Studies have demonstrated that these frequencies affect our physical realities. Be kind to yourself and others.

Toxic Chemicals contribute to the chronic disease of 33M Americans. Its the biggest culprit of lowering our vibe. Its in our water, food, skin care.

Alcohol & *Caffeine*: the more free you are from addictions of every kind, the more in control you have over your energy and your vibe.

RAISES VIBE

RAISES AND LOWERS VIBE

LOWERS VIBE

CHAPTER *12*

We are spiritual beings having a human experience.

PIERRE TEILHARD DE CHARDIN

What is normal

Why be normal? Normal is boring! Normal really means: I'm trying to be like everyone else. To have the same experiences as everyone else. The best thing you can do is stop comparing *your experiences* to the experiences of others. That's when things get all mucked up (excuse my French). Let me tell you why.

- We are only and always translating energy.
- What we see, hear, taste, and smell is us translating vibration through our physical senses (as seen on the following page).
- Therefore, there's no such thing as normal.
- How and what you translate is *real* for you.
- It's *irrelevant* if it is or isn't real for someone else.

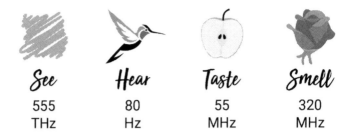

See	Hear	Taste	Smell
555 THz	80 Hz	55 MHz	320 MHz

You see the color green because your eyes are translating light waves that are vibrating at 555 THz per second. You hear a hummingbird because your ears are translating the sound wave that is vibrating at 80 Hz per second. Our senses are translating mechanisms. They exist to translate energy.

- That's why you hear yanny and I hear laurel.
- That's why you see blue and I see green.
- That's why you say potato and I say potahto (just kidding, no one says potahto – *that's* not normal.)
- For this reason, you should not compare your experiences to the experiences of others.
- Instead, get really curious about why you are translating the energy in this way.
- It is important, particularly as a Reiki practitioner, to get used to translating energy and to know what it means for *you*.
- Let me give you a personal example.
- This example is as much about intuition as it is about translating energy and so the story serves two purposes.

About a year ago, a new Reiki client was referred to me. I knew nothing about her and she knew nothing about me. I gave her a client form to fill out, as I do with all new clients. On the client form, there is a space to share information about what ailments you want treated. She didn't fill this part out, which is ideal for me; the less I know the easier it is for me to hold the space of wellbeing. (I know you remember this from Chapter 2.) During the session, almost right away, *my* upper lip began to twitch. This type of reaction in my body had never happened to me in my previous years of practicing on clients. I didn't know exactly what it meant and, at first, I thought maybe my upper lip is *just* twitching. I had been doing this long enough, however, to know that the twitching that I felt in my upper lip was me translating the energy in *her* body, not mine. The twitching continued for the entire session and then stopped as soon as the session concluded. Before the woman left, I said to her, "I don't know if this will mean anything to you, but my upper lip was twitching the entire session." She looked at me (kind of like I had two heads) and politely said, "No, it doesn't mean anything to me." She left. I left.

I didn't give much thought to it, until a week later, when she emailed me. She wrote that she thought it was weird that I would say that to her. So, she did what any of us would do; she googled 'What does it mean when your upper lip is twitching?' (I'll save you the trouble.) What she found is that a person's upper lip will often twitch when she is releasing emotional trauma. I didn't know it at the time of her session, but she shared that the reason why she came to me for Reiki was to assist with releasing some emotional resistance in her life. As she was lying on the Reiki table, she was indeed releasing many emotions that were stored in her body, which were no longer serving her. As she released, I translated this energy as a twitch in my upper lip. I could have easily chalked this up to nothing, and if I did, it probably wouldn't have made a difference either way. Another Reiki practitioner may have translated this energy in a very different way and *neither would be wrong or less accurate.* The point is: we are all connected. If we are mindful, we can feel and translate these subtle energies in a meaningful way.

What's *normal* when it comes to the Reiki attunements

- Let's explore what experiences you *might* have during the attunement process.
- What happens during a Reiki attunement is unique for every individual.
- Remember, there is no *normal.*
- You must understand what is happening during the Reiki attunement process.
- During the attunement, the student is connected to the Reiki source and alterations are being made in the student's energy pathways to accommodate the changes needed for Reiki.
- The adjustments that are being made are specifically for *your* highest good.
- For some, it can be a bit uncomfortable.
- I've had students tell me that they feel nauseous right after (or during) an attunement.
- The majority of my students talk about a feeling of peace or unconditional love.
- Some see colors or beams of light.
- Some see objects or even people.
- Some feel like they're floating.

- The reason why each experience is unique is because you are *translating* the Reiki energy as it begins to make the alterations in *your* energy pathways.
- Alterations are different for each person because each person has led a different life.
- The only thing I know for sure is that after an attunement, you will be *pulled* toward a life of growth and transformation.
- The degree to which you follow this *pull* is up to you.
- Some may choose not to follow it at all.
- Others, like you, are up for the ride.

CHAPTER 13

If you've heard nothing else, hear this

Here's what my heart wants to scream from the top of the tallest mountain.

- You are worthy!
- You are loved!
- You can trust your inner-voice above all else!
- You are unique and your wellness journey, including your Reiki practice, should be unique too. Don't copy what I say. Don't copy *my* path. Speak your truth from your *own* heart.
- Don't give a crap about what anyone else thinks. Usually - if not always - what others have to say is more about themselves and the stuff that's going on in their *own* lives/heads.
- You have the power to change everything in your life.

- If you bring your vibration above 62 MHz by consistently focusing on lifestyle choices in all four levels (Chapter 4), you will be high-flying and have access to the life of your dreams.
- Don't take any of this too seriously.
- Be eager for what's to come.
- None of us get out of here *alive*.
- So, instead of trying to avoid the inevitable – live, love, and spread good vibes.

In case you haven't figured it out yet, I'm not a person who believes that Reiki is the answer to all of your problems. I also don't believe it will cure all of your ailments (for most people). Instead, I believe that Reiki *starts* the journey. Where you go from here is up to you. How exciting!

Conclusion: be a lamp, a lifeboat, a ladder

I love my Reiki clients. I love spending an hour with them in a deep meditative state. I love that I can be the person that holds that space of wellbeing for them. I love that I can see the shift in their energy towards alignment. I love that when I test their chakras after a session, every-single-dang-time, I see the evidence of that alignment.

What I love even more, is when people give the gift of Reiki to *themselves*. Teaching students Reiki, passing on Reiki through the attunement process, watching faces light up during class when students get a glimpse of their inner truth, hearing about their transformation as they journey through the three levels...that's why I do what I do.

My ultimate purpose for creating this book is to bring the story of Reiki to more people with the hope that they may want to take this path for themselves. I believe EVERYONE can benefit from being attuned to Reiki and learning about Reiki. It is a powerful tool that can raise your vibration (and the vibration of everything around you) on a consistent basis. I imagine what this world would be like if everyone understood the connection we have, not only with each other, but with the Divine. Know that you can be your own *greatest healer* and, in doing so, the world becomes healed, one person at a time.

Until we meet again – sending love, Reiki, and good vibes.
Namaste,

Cortney

Acknowledgments

Love

My husband – **Brian** - who has supported me, my crazy ideas and, most importantly, my evolution for 20+ years. He is my rock. My sound board. My safe place to fall. I love you always.

My family – **Bob, Brenda, Heather** and **Nikki** – they loved me when I was unlovable, took care of me when I was at my lowest. They are the epitome of unconditional love. I love you always.

My best friends – **Amy, Danielle, Julie** and **Stephanie** – four of the strongest women I know, and my tribe that would have my back under any and all circumstances. I love you always. #fabfive

My son – **Zach** – who inspires my connection to the Divine. I love you always.

Reiki

There would be no Reiki in my life without the guidance of my

Reiki Master, **Susan**.

Also, my yoga teacher, **Larry**.

Deep appreciation for my Reiki students and clients, who have inspired this book.

Vibration

Deepest gratitude to my countless spiritual teachers who continue to raise my vibration.

Dianne, Rashel, and **Ted** who spoke faith into me and gave me the courage to live my dreams, so many years ago.

And **Raquel**, who still whispers guidance even after her transition.

Lastly, special shout-out to my yoga community and **Yoga Squared.**

Collaboration

Editor – **Heather Ninni**

Book cover, graphics and formatting – **SHINE Akron LLC**, design

In your light, I learn how to love. In your beauty, how to make poems. You dance inside my chest where no-one sees you, but sometimes I do, and that sight becomes this art.

Rumi

Love

INTERESTING FACTS ABOUT LOVE

- Sanskrit has 96 words for love; ancient Persian has 80, Greek has three, and English only has one.
- When two people who love each other look into each other's eyes, their heart rates become synchronized.
- Simply looking at a picture of a loved one relieves pain you might feel in the body.
- Holding a loved one's hand relieves stress.
- Love influences creativity.
- Love can literally make you stronger. That's why a mother can lift a car off of her trapped child.
- The sound frequency of love is 528 HZ.
- The emotion of love is 500 MHz, just slightly below peace and enlightenment.
- Love is the key to healing.

You cannot teach a man anything; you can only help him find it within himself.

Galileo

REIKI

INTERESTING FACTS ABOUT REIKI

- Reiki is a Japanese healing technique that promotes wellbeing.
- The word Reiki comes from two Japanese words and means life force energy guided by Source.
- A practitioner administers Reiki by gently laying hands on another or oneself.
- Reiki is transferred during an attunement process from an experienced Reiki Master to a student.
- During the attunement, the student is connected to the Reiki source and alterations are being made in the student's energy pathways to accommodate the changes needed for Reiki.
- In its history, since 1914, Reiki has aided in healing virtually every known illness.
- Scientifically speaking, this happens because Reiki increases the frequency of the human body.
- The medical community has begun to embrace Reiki.
- There are well-over two million Reiki practitioners and 300,000 Reiki Masters practicing today.

If you want to find the secrets of the universe, think in terms of energy, frequency, and vibration.

Nikola Tesla

vibration

INTERESTING FACTS ABOUT VIBRATION

- Albert Einstein said, "Everything in life is vibration."
- What Einstein meant is that every atom in every molecule oscillates and is in motion and can be measured.
- Vibrations can be felt and translated with our five senses.
- There are wellness implications in relation to your personal frequency (vibration).
- Often vibration is measured in the form of hertz.
- Scientific studies have measured the frequencies of the human body.
- The frequency range of a healthy human body lies within 62-72 MHz.
- When frequency begins to drop, we are receptive to colds and flus around 57-60 MHz.
- Anything below 58 MHz, causes us to become receptive to diseases, including cancer around 42 MHz.
- At 25 MHz, death begins to occur.
- According to studies, every disease has a frequency.
- Certain frequencies can prevent the development of disease and can even destroy disease.
- In theory, if we keep the frequencies of our bodies above 62 MHz, diseases and harmful microorganisms would have a very hard time surviving in our bodies.
- Everything we eat, think, consume, ingest, and experience contributes to our own personal frequency.
- Reiki, love, and gratitude are the quickest ways to raise your personal frequency and therefore kick-start your wellbeing.

About the author

Cortney Martinelli is a Reiki Master, CYT, Visual Communication Designer, and the founder of SHINE Akron LLC. She has been supporting the Reiki community since 2010. Before this, she wasn't a very happy person. In fact, she was pretty miserable. Her dark times led her to radical growth and a personal mission to share peace, joy, and wellbeing with others. There was no roadmap, so she stumbled, fell, and picked herself back up again. She blindly tried anything and everything to arrive at an imaginary place of peace, joy, and wellbeing. Today, it is no longer imaginary - it is reality. It's not by luck or chance, it's science; and she gladly shares her learnings with you.

Cortney's mission with SHINE is to collaborate with other souls; bring their passion to life; and encourage and empower

Photo credit: Elizabeth Tipton

them to share it with others - SHINE! She strives to do this through her classes, workshops, books, Reiki sessions, Reiki training, yoga, chemical-free skin care, and enlightened design.

Cortney lives in Akron, Ohio with her husband, Brian; son, Zach; and dog, Jasper. Most of her days are spent in her office overlooking her beautiful three-acre property in the middle of the city that she loves. When she isn't working, this self-proclaimed home-body enjoys spending time with her family, practicing yoga and binge-watching Netflix.

Visit www.shineakron.com to learn more and to find opportunities to co-create in the future.

This book was *guided* by Reiki.

Shanti
Shanti
Shanti
Peace in the mind
Peace in the body
Peace in the spirit

All-ways
Namaste

Made in the USA
Columbia, SC
28 September 2020